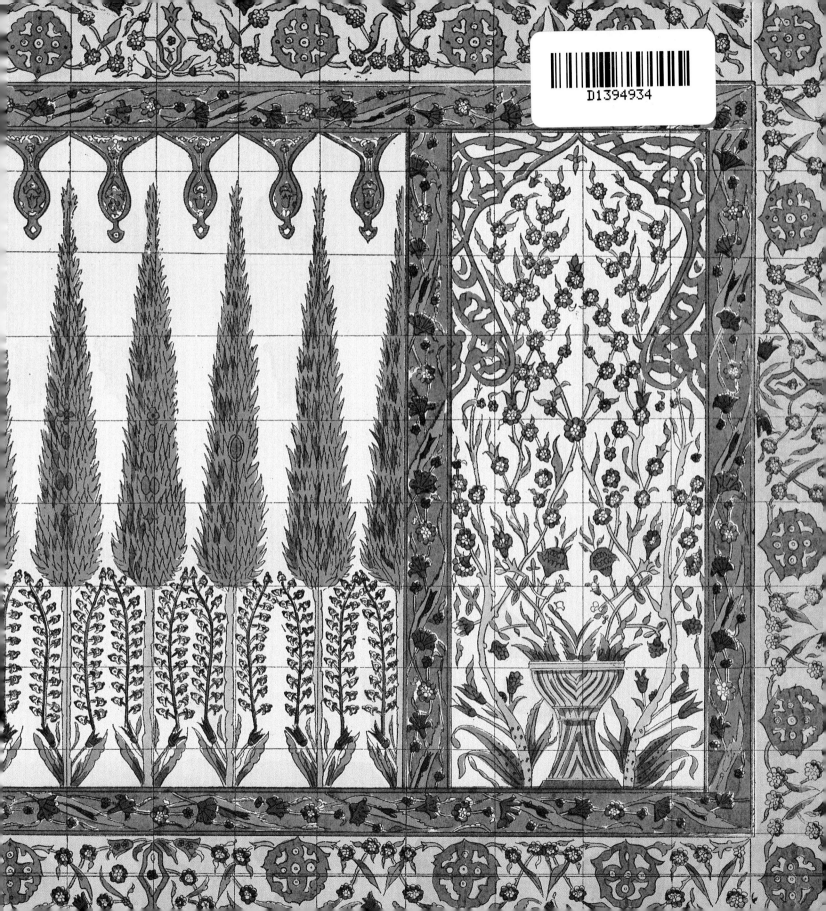

THE PERFUMED GARDEN

SIR RICHARD BURTON

EDITED AND INTRODUCED BY
CHARLES FOWKES

PHOTOGRAPHED BY LANCE DANE

HAMLYN

ACKNOWLEDGEMENTS

It would not have been possible to produce this first illustrated edition of The Perfumed Garden without the generous co-operation of VICTOR LOWNES, CHHOTU SHARMA, BRUNO JEAN and LANCE DANE, who have allowed paintings from their collections to be reproduced. The jacket subjects are reproduced by courtesy of the Trustees of the Victoria and Albert Museum.

This book is dedicated to the memory of Shrí OM PRAKASH SHARMA — a fine artist.

First published in 1989 by
The Hamlyn Publishing Group Limited,
a division of The Octopus Publishing Group,
Michelin House, 81 Fulham Road,
London SW3 6RB.

Copyright © Charles Fowkes 1989

ISBN 0 600 564 231

Printed in Italy By Sagdos, Milan.

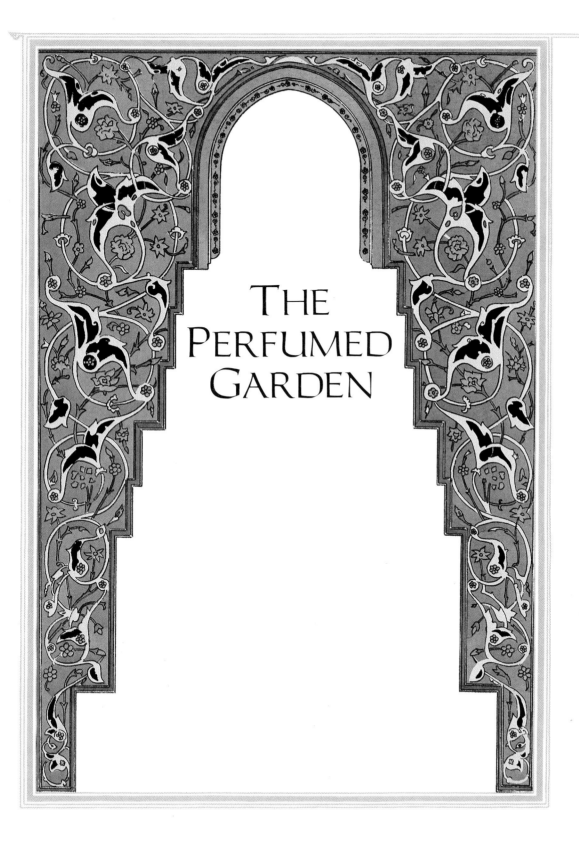

THE
PERFUMED
GARDEN

INTRODUCTION

I

Sir Richard Francis Burton, KCMG, died on Monday October 20th 1890. With cruelly judged irony, The Destroyer of Delights and Sunderer of Societies surprised the restless soul of the traveller and man of action in the bedroom of his home in Trieste where he was the British Consul. While his native country indulged in its all too frequent habit of honouring and praising after death those it ill-treats and neglects in life, Trieste society — from the humblest to the highest — prepared to show its genuine respect for the world famous explorer, linguist and writer who had spent his last eighteen years amongst them.

Richard Burton's wife and literary executor Isabel, 'alone and desolate forever', locked herself in the study of the man who had been her 'earthly God for thirty-five years'. For sixteen days she read the manuscripts and personal diaries which her husband had left in her hands. She laboured day and night at the daunting task in the certain knowledge that only hard work could prevent grief from totally overwhelming her. While Isabel sifted through the huge volume of accumulated paper, messages of condolence began to arrive from around the world. Among them was a telegram from the English publisher Leonard Smithers offering Richard Burton's widow — whose financial position was precarious — the then enormous sum of six thousand guineas for the manuscript which her husband had 'finished the day before he died.

For some time Burton had been aware that his iron constitution was at last failing and death was not far away. In order to provide for his wife he had revised and annotated a sixteenth-century Arab manuscript which he had translated several years before, and had published through the Kama Shastra Society. (The Society was a smokescreen designed to avoid prosecution because its publications, though scholarly and of the highest quality, were unashamedly erotic). In its earlier form this work — known as The Perfumed Garden — had sold extremely well. Burton knew that with the addition of his ethnological notes on the sexual practices of the Arabs, and with the missing chapter dealing with homosexuality re-instated, The Perfumed Garden would provide sufficient income to keep Isabel in comfort for the rest of her life. The offer from Smithers shows that his judgement in this matter was correct. But although Isabel read the telegram she made no reply.

On the sixteenth day after the death of her husband, Isabel made a series of trips from the study to the garden of the spacious villa where they had had their home together. Each successive trip was slower and more difficult that the last: she was devastated by grief, exhausted from more than two weeks of intense concentration and in pain from the illness which would eventually kill her. But she refused all assistance until she had amassed a large bonfire. The fire which Isabel ignited that day was a holocaust: it burned all Richard Burton's private diaries, and most of his journals, notebooks and letters; it burned the entire manuscript of The Perfumed Garden, more than a thousand pages; it burned Isabel Burton's reputation — and it still burns today.

II

There is not room here to explore Isabel Burton's motives for the burning in detail, but although it does not compensate us for the loss, or excuse the terrible act — God knows she has paid for that destruction. All the good that Isabel did in dedicating her life to one of the most remarkable — and difficult — men of the nineteenth century has been forgotten because of the burning. She nursed his body through several near fatal illnesses, and nursed his mind through repeated bouts of depression and self-destructive behaviour. She was always devoted to him and he became equally devoted to her. In the atmosphere created by Isabel he was able to produce the greatest of all his achievements — the ten volumes of The Arabian Nights.

The burning of books is such a sinister and dangerous business that even the temperature at which they ignite (Fahrenheit 451) has been made a potent cypher for evil. In our horror at the idea of burning any books, especially those of a significant writer such as Burton, we should not forget that Isabel enabled the creation of more and greater books than she ever destroyed. There was also a ghastly hypocrisy in the vilification she suffered after his death at the hands of those who would have never dreamed of reading a book as frankly erotic as The Perfumed Garden had it survived.

Whatever her reasons for the burning — and they were certainly not those most frequently levelled at her — Isabel Burton knew the price she would be made to pay for her actions. 'Let the world rain fire and brimstone on me now', she said. And she did not exaggerate.

III

Although we will never know what Richard Burton made of the greatly enlarged and annotated version of The Perfumed Garden which perished in the flames in Trieste, we can still enjoy the earlier version first published in 1886. Working from a French translation, Burton transformed his material through his unique knowledge of the customs and attitudes of the Arabs. He was the greatest Arabist of his time and his profound knowledge of the rhythms of Arab life and literature enabled him to translate Sheikh Nefzawi's original in the fullest sense. The Perfumed Garden is not great literature in the way that 'The Book of the Thousand Nights and a Night' is, but

Burton brought all the same scholarship to it. Perhaps because it is less awesome and monumental than 'The Nights' — although several stories are common to both — he felt he could be more free with his subject. The Perfumed Garden (Men's Hearts to Gladden) enabled Richard Burton to combine his scholarship, his ferocious interest in all aspects of sex and his mordant humour all in one vehicle. The result is a remarkable book.

The Perfumed Garden (in some manuscripts The Scented Garden) was written by the shadowy figure Sheikh Nefzawi in the early sixteenth century. He tells us himself that it was written as a commission for the Grand Vizier of Tunis, and there is a hint that it was prepared not only to ingratiate himself but to atone for some unspecified misdemeanour. Sheikh Nefzawi's problems may have been financial or political —they were unstable times in North Africa — but the result is an urbane, humorous, tongue-in-cheek (and everywhere else) confection.

In many respects Sheikh Nefzawi and Richard Burton are kindred spirits. Both were men of action: in addition to book learning there is clearly a great deal of first-hand experience in their descriptions of sexual behaviour. Both men relish the way in which humour can illuminate and entertain: it is difficult to tell whether author or translator had more fun with the descriptions of the self-importance and vulnerability of the male organ in its various aspects. There is also a shared relish for shocking.

The Perfumed Garden is very different from the earlier publications of the Kama Shastra Society, such as Ananga Ranga and Kama Sutra. Although the abbreviation necessary for reasons of space in the present edition has provided a welcome opportunity for the more sexist and racist stories to be omitted, it is very clear that The Perfumed Garden was not written with the same pious intention as the Hindu love manuals. There is good sexual advice in The Perfumed Garden — the importance of foreplay, of expressions of tenderness such as kissing — but it is closer in intention to the eighteenth-century 'aphrodisiac' writing of John Cleland and Mirabeau than the clinical aphorisms of Kama Sutra. In style, The Perfumed Garden is closer still to the bawdy tales of Boccaccio or Chaucer which explore the humorous possibilities of sexual appetite in action, while making a few sly points along the way.

The joint-founder of the Kama Shastra Society, F.F. Arbuthnot, had little to do with the publication of The Perfumed Garden. His main interest was sexual education, which he knew could be helped by making available in the West the great works of Hindu erotology with their emphasis on equality and the needs of the woman. Although Arbuthnot (known affectionately as 'Bunny') remained Burton's closest friend, the publication of the first volume of the Arabian Nights in 1885 marked a change of direction.

The Kama Shastra Society was now Richard Burton's publishing vehicle. He used it to explore the byways of literary erotica with Leonard Smithers and he used it to publish the fabulous Arabian Nights. It was not only commercial opportunism which led to the

publication of The Perfumed Garden in 1886 when the furore surrounding The Arabian Nights was at its height. Certainly anything about the Arab world from the hand of Richard Burton was going to sell — and it did. But there were other forces at work. Why give time to a minor classic when you are in the middle of publishing the ten volumes of a major literary work — the most important achievement of your career? Burton could certainly spend money, but he cared little for it. Perhaps The Perfumed Garden was a recreation, a piece of work where he could be less guarded and more spontaneous. There is an unmistakeable sense of being very close to the author when you read the book. The shadowy figure of 'Sheikh Nefzawi' may be less to do with the original author and more to do with the translator's subconscious. Burton was a sensitive and analytical writer who would have recognized what had happened. It is possible that in choosing to revise and expand the same text in what he knew to be his last work, Richard Burton intended to reveal himself more than he had ever done. Perhaps that is why Isabel burned it.

Charles Fowkes

Praise be to God who has placed the source of man's greatest pleasure in woman's natural parts, and woman's greatest pleasure in the natural parts of man!

Who has decreed that the well-being, satisfaction and comfort of a woman's parts shall depend on the welcome they accord to the virile member, and that a man shall know neither rest nor peace till his duty has been nobly done!

When the mutual operation is performed, a lively combat ensues between the two actors who frolic and kiss and intertwine. Enjoyment is not long delayed, in consequence of the contact of the two pubes. Man, in the pride of his strength, works like a pestle, and woman, with lascivious undulations, comes artfully to his aid. Soon, all too soon, the ejaculation comes!

God has granted us the kiss on the mouth, the cheeks and the neck, as also the sucking of luscious lips, to provoke an erection at a favourable time. It is He, who, in His wisdom, has embellished with breasts a woman's chest, her neck with a double chin, and her cheeks with jewels and brilliants. He has also given her eyes which inspire love, and lashes sharp as polished blades. With admirable flanks and a delightful navel He has heightened the beauty of her gently domed belly. He has endowed her with buttocks nobly planned, and has supported the whole on majestic thighs. Between these latter He has placed the field of strife which, when it abounds in flesh, resembles by its amplitude a lion's head. Its name among mankind is 'vulva'. Oh, how innumerable are the men who have died for this! how many, alas, of the bravest!

God has given this object a mouth, a tongue, two lips and a shape like unto the footprint of a gazelle on the sands of the desert.

All this is supported by two wonderful columns, witnesses to the power and wisdom of God; they are neither too long nor too short, and are ornamented with knees and calves, and ankles on which jewels repose. The Almighty has plunged woman into a sea of splendour, voluptuousness and delight; he has clothed her in precious raiment, and brightened her face with smiles.

Let praise be given to God that He has created woman with her beauty and appetizing flesh: that He has endowed her with hair, waist, and throat, breasts which swell, and amorous gestures which increase desire.

The Master of the Universe has given them a power of seduction over all men: weak or strong, without distinction, fall under the spell of their love. Communal life depends on women: it is they who decide for sojourn or dispersion.

The state of humility of the hearts of those who love but who are separated from the object of their affection; fires their breasts with the flames of love; it loads them with submissiveness, contempt and misery, and betrays them into all manner of vicissitudes as a consequence of their passion; and all that as the result of an ardent desire for union.

I, a servant of God, render thanks to Him that no man can withstand the charms of a beautiful woman, that no man can free himself from the desire of possession.

I testify that there is no other God but GOD himself, and that He has no partner! This testimony I carefully make in view of the Last Judgment.

I also bear witness to our Lord and Master MOHAMMED, the Servant of God and Lord of the Prophets (may the blessing and mercy of God be showered on him and his!) I reserve my prayers and benedictions for the day of retribution — God grant they be heard!

History of the present work

I have based this work on a small book dealing with the mysteries of generation, entitled 'The Torch of the Universe', which had been brought to the notice of the Vizier of our Lord ABD EL AZIZ, master of Tunis, the well-protected. The illustrious Vizier was his poet, companion, friend, and private secretary. He was judicious, well-tried, sagacious and wise, the most learned of all the men of his time, and the one whose opinion was most often sought. His name was Mohammed ben Ouana ez Zouaoui, and he belonged to the tribe of the Zouaouas. He had been brought up at Algiers, and it was here that he made the acquaintance of our Lord Abd el Aziz el Hafsi. On the day of the Spanish conquest of Algiers (1510) our Lord fled with him to Tunis (may God in His might preserve him to the Resurrection Day!) and there elected him to the post of Grand Vizier.

When the afore-mentioned work came into his hands, he sent me a pressing invitation to visit him. I immediately went to his dwelling where he received me with the greatest kindness. Three days later he came to me and showed me my little book, and said:

'This is your work!'

Seeing that I blushed, he added:

'You have no cause for shame, for all you have written is quite true; there is nothing in it to frighten anyone. Besides, you are not the first to treat of these matters, and, I swear by God, the knowledge contained in this book should be widely known. It is only the ignorant and fearful who will avoid it or try to turn it to ridicule. But there are still a few things you ought to say.'

I asked him what they were.

'Oh, master!' I replied, 'all that you ask will be easy to perform if the work find favour in the sight of God.'

I immediately set to work to compile the treatise, imploring the aid of God (may He shower His blessings on His prophet, and grant us salvation and mercy!)

I have entitled my book The Perfumed Garden for the Repose of the Mind.

And I asked God who has arranged everything for our good (and there is only one God, and all good things come from Him!) to aid me with His support and to lead me into the right pathway. Our strength and happiness rest in God, the Almighty and All-highest!

CONCERNING PRAISEWORTHY MEN

Learn, Oh Vizier (may the blessing of God rest on you), that men and women are of divers kinds; some there are who are worthy of praise, while others deserve only censure.

When a worthy man is in the company of women his member grows, becomes strong, vigorous and hard; he is slow to ejaculate and, after the spasm caused by the emission of semen, he is prompt at re-erection.

Such a man is relished and appreciated by women, for they only love man for his sex. His member then must be well-developed: his chest should be light and his buttocks strong: he should be slow to ejaculate but quick to erect: his member should reach to the bottom of the vagina in which it should be a snug fit.

A man so endowed will be dearly cherished.

Qualities which Women look for in Men

It is related that on a certain day Abd el Melik ben Merouan sought out his mistress Leilla and asked her questions concerning many things. Among others he asked her what qualities a woman looks for in a man.

She answered:
'Oh, master, they must have cheeks like ours.'

'And what else?'

'Hair like ours; in fact they must resemble thee, oh Prince of Believers; for verily if a man be not rich and powerful he will have no success with women.'

Concerning the length of the virile member

For a virile member to be pleasing to a woman its length should be, at most, three hand-breadths, and, at least, one hand-breadth and a half. The man whose member is less than two-breadths long will enjoy but indifferent success.

ON THE UTILITY OF SCENTS IN COITION

The story of Mosailama

Scents have the power of exciting sexual desires in both man and woman. When a woman inhales the scent with which a man is perfumed she loses her power of control, and it will often be found that man has here a powerful means of gaining possession of a woman.

Touching this matter, it is related that Mosailama the imposter, son of Kais (whom God curse!) claimed to have the gift of prophecy, and that he imitated the Prophet of God (may blessings and salvation rest upon him!). On this account he and a great number of Arabs have incurred the anger of the Almighty.

Mosailama falsified the Koran by his lies and impostures, and, touching the chapter of the Koran which the angel Gabriel (God grant him salvation!) brought to the Prophet (the mercy of God be with him!) it is said that when some evil men came to Mosailama, he said to them: 'The angel Gabriel brought me a similar chapter.'

Now learn what happened to that woman of the Beni-Temim whose name was Sheja et Temimia and who claimed to prophesy: she had heard speak of Mosailama and he had heard speak of her.

This woman was powerful, for the Beni-Temim were a numerous tribe. She said: 'It is not meet that two persons should prophesy. Either he must be prophet and then I and my disciples will follow his laws, or I must be prophet and he and his disciples must follow mine.'

This happened after the death of the True Prophet, (on whom be the blessing of God!)

Sheja then wrote to Mosailama the following letter: It is not meet that two persons should prophesy simultaneously, but only one; we will meet and examine our doctrines, we and our disciples. We will discuss that which God has revealed to us, and we will follow the laws of the one who is judged to be the true prophet.

She then closed the letter and gave it to a courier, saying. 'Take this message to el Yamama and give it to Mosailama ben Kais; meanwhile, I will follow with my army.'

The next day the prophetess mounted her horse and, accompanied by her suite, followed in the steps of her envoy. When the latter reached Mosailama he greeted him and presented the letter.

Mosailama opened it, read it, and grasped its import; he was dismayed by the message and immediately took counsel of his suite, but they were unable to advise him. While he was thus perplexed one of his chief followers approached him and said:

'Oh, Mosailama, calm your mind and refresh your eyes. I am going to advise you as a father would a son.'

'Speak, and let your words be sincere,' replied Mosailama.

'Tomorrow morning let a tent of coloured brocade be raised on the outskirts of the town, and let it be richly furnished. Fill it then with delicious perfumes of various kinds, amber, musk, and scented flowers such as the rose, orange-blossom, jonquil, jasmine, hyacinth, pink, and others similar. That done, you will place in the tent golden cassolettes filled with perfumes, such as green aloes, ambergris, nedde, and other pleasant odours. Then the tent must be closed that none of the perfume can escape, and when the vapours have become sufficiently intense to impregnate the water which is in the tent, you will mount your throne and send for the prophetess, who will remain in the tent with you alone. When she inhales the perfumes she will be delighted, all her joints will slacken and she will swoon away. After having possessed her you will be spared further trouble from her.'

'Your advice is good,' exclaimed Mosailama. 'By God! it's a fine idea!'

He then took steps to put the plan in practice. As soon as he saw that the vapours were intense enough to impregnate the water in the tent, he mounted his throne and sent for the prophetess. When he saw her drawing near he ordered her to be shown into the tent. She entered and, when they were alone, he spoke to her. While he was speaking she began to lose her presence of mind; she seemed thunderstruck and stupefied.

When he saw her in this state he knew that she desired coition, so he said:

'Get up, so that I may possess you, for this place has been prepared for that purpose. If you desire it you may lie on your back, go on all fours, or take up the position used in prayer, with your head on the ground and your buttocks in the air like a tripod. Whatever posture you prefer, speak, and you shall be satisfied.'

'I want it all ways,' replied the prophetess. 'Let the revelation of God enter within me, oh Prophet of the Almighty!'

He at once fell upon her and enjoyed her as he would, after which she said:

'When I go out from here, ask me in marriage of my suite.'

She then left the tent and went to her disciples who asked her the result of the conference. She replied:

'Mosailama has shown me all that has been revealed to him, and I know it to be the truth: obey him!'

Mosailama asked her in marriage and the request was granted. When the disciples asked him about the future bride's dowry, he replied:

'I exempt you from saying the afternoon prayer.'

When the Beni-Temim are now asked why they do not say this prayer, they reply:

'Because of our prophetess; she alone knows the way of truth.' And verily they acknowledge no other prophet but she.

The death of Mosailama was announced by the prophecy of Abou Beker (may God favour him!) He was, in fact, killed by Zeidben Khettab; others say by Ouhsha, one of his disciples.

As to Sheja, she repented and became a Musselman. Later she married a follower of the Prophet (may the Lord look with favour on her husband!).

Thus ends the story.

For a man to be successful with women he must pay them marked attention. His dress should be neat, his figure graceful, and his looks should mark him out from his fellows. He must be truthful and sincere, generous and brave. He should not be vain, and he should make himself agreeable in company. He must be the slave of his word; if he makes a promise he must keep it; he must always speak the truth and never fail to perform whatever he undertakes. He who boasts of his relations with women is contemptible.

On the Importance of Humour

The Story of Bahloul

It is related that there was once a king named Mamoun who had a jester named Bahloul. One day, wishing to give Bahloul a proof of his kindness, he made him a present of a gold-embroidered robe, the finest of all his garments.

Bahloul went off in high spirits in the direction of the Grand Vizier's. Now it so happened that the beautiful Hamdouna caught sight of him from the roof of her palace. She said to her servant:

'By the God of the Temple and of Mecca! Behold Bahloul dressed in a beautiful golden robe: by what stratagem could I obtain possession of it?'

'Oh, mistress, you will never be able to get that robe,' said the servant.

'I have thought of a ruse by which I can get it,' replied Hamdouna.

'Bahloul is a cunning fellow,' said the servant. 'Many think they can trick him, but he tricks them instead. Give up your plan, dear mistress, for fear you should fall into the trap you set for him.

'No I intend to try,' replied Hamdouna.

'So she sent her attendant to Bahloul to ask him to come to her. He willingly consented.

Hamdouna greeted him and said:

'Oh, Bahloul, I believe you have come here to hear me sing.'

'Assuredly, my mistress,' replied he; for Hamdouna had a wonderful gift for singing.

'I suppose that after you have heard me sing you would be willing to take some refreshment?'

'Yes,' replied he.

She then began to sing in a wonderful manner, and all those who heard her could have died for love.

After Bahloul had listened to her songs she had refreshments brought for him. He ate and drank, and she said to him:

19

'I don't know what has made me think you would willingly give me your robe.'

'Oh, mistress mine, I have taken an oath that I will only give it to her with whom I have done what a man does to a woman.'

'What! you know what that is, Bahloul?'

'Why not?' replied he: 'I who instruct all men on this matter. It is I who join them in love; who teach them the pleasures that woman yields; how they must caress, and what are the things which excite and satisfy. Who, indeed, should understand copulation, if not I?'

Now Hamdouna was Mamoun's daughter, and wife of the Grand Vizier. She was endowed with perfect beauty, and her graceful figure dazzled the beholder. She was by far the most beautiful woman of her time. If a hero saw her he become humble and submissive, and dropped his eyes to escape temptation. If any man looked on her he was sorely tried, and even Bahloul had hitherto avoided her for fear that he might fall. She had sent for him several times before, but he feared for his repose, so this was his first time with her.

Bahloul began to chat with her; at times he looked at her and at times he cast down his eyes, for he feared he might lose control of his passion. Hamdouna was burning with desire to get the robe, but he was determined not to give it up unless she paid his price.

'What is your price?' she asked.

'Coition, oh apple of my eye!'

'You understand the business?'

'No one understands women better than I. I know what they like; for learn, oh mistress, that in this world men take up various occupations in accordance with their tastes. This one takes, that one gives; this one sells, that one buys. But none of those things attracts me. My sole thought is of love and the possession of beautiful women. I heal those who are suffering through love, and bring relief to thirsting vulvas.'

When Hamdouna heard these words she became excited and curiously examined Bahloul's member which had proudly raised its head. First she thought: 'I'll give in'; then: 'I'll refuse him.' However, while she was hesitating she had a sense of pleasure 'twixt her thighs, for the liquid forerunner of love had begun to flow. She could no longer resist the thought of copulation, so she quietened her fears by saying that no one would believe Bahloul should he boast of his victory over her. She then asked him to take off his robe and enter the chamber, but Bahloul replied:

'I shall only take it off when I have satisfied my desire, oh apple of my eye!'

Trembling with passion, Hamdouna stood up, undid her girdle, and left the room.

Bahloul followed her, saying to himself: 'Am I awake or do I dream?'

When they arrived at her dressing-room she flung herself on a silken canopied bed, and, trembling all over, she drew her robe up over her thighs till all that God had given her that was beautiful was revealed to Bahloul's eyes. He examined her belly which was elegantly domed, and let his gaze rest on her navel which looked like a pearl in a golden bowl, but, when he let his eyes travel lower, he saw a wonderful creation and well-turned thighs of dazzling white.

Then he clasped Hamdouna in a passionate embrace and soon saw all animation fade from her face. She sank beneath him, clasping his member in her hands and exciting it with her fires. Then Bahloul said:

'Why are you so troubled and outside of yourself?'

'Peace, oh son of debauchery. I am like a mare in heat and you still excite me with your words. And what words! They would tempt the purest woman on earth. Do you wish to kill me with your words?'

'Am I not like your husband?'

'Yes, but a woman gets in heat for any man, whether he be her husband or no, as a mare does through any stallion. There is this difference however: a mare is only excited by a stallion at certain times of the year and it is only then that she receives him, whereas a woman can always be excited with passionate words of love. That explains my attitude towards you, so do not delay for my husband will soon return.'

'Oh, my mistress, my loins are weak and I cannot mount upon your breast; you mount on me and act the man's part, then take my robe and I'll depart.'

That said, he lay down in the position usually occupied by the woman, and his staff reared its head between his thighs.

Then Hamdouna threw herself upon Bahloul, seized his member, and scrutinized it carefully. She was amazed at its size and magnificent shape, and its strength and hardness delighted her.

'Behold the cause of woman's downfall, and the source of many troubles. Oh, Bahloul, I have never seen a sturdier specimen.'

However, she continued holding it and rubbed its head against the lips of her natural parts with such effect that soon it began to weep. And then her vulva seemed to say: 'Oh, member, enter in!'

Then Bahloul introduced his penis into the vagina of the Sultan's daughter, and she, lowering at the same time her croup on to the tool, caused it to sink completely into the furnace. Nothing remained outside, not even the smallest trace could be seen, and she cried: 'How debauched are women, and how tireless has God made them in their pursuit of pleasure!' She then began to move backwards and forwards like a sieve at work, and surely never before were such graceful movements seen. This she continued till Bahloul's cup of joy was filled. The blissful moment soon arrived, for the clinging embrace of her vagina seemed to pump Bahloul's member as if it sucked it, as an infant sucks its mother's breast. Enjoyment came to both at the same time, and each felt well repaid.

Then Hamdouna caught hold of the member to withdraw it, which she did with caressing care; looking at it she said: 'That is the mark of a valorous man!' She then wiped it and herself on a silken handkerchief, and afterwards stood up.

Bahloul also got up and started to walk away, but she said:

'What about the robe?'

'What, you have had the privilege of riding me and now you want a present!'

'But did you not say that you could not mount me because of the pains in your loins?'

'No matter!' replied Bahloul, 'the first time was for you, the second will be for me; that is the price of the robe, then I'll go away.'

Hamdouna thought to herself: 'Since he has begun he may as well keep on, then he will go away.'

With this idea she lay down, but Bahloul said: 'I shall not lie down with you unless you take off all your clothing.'

So she took of all her clothing and Bahloul went into exstasy at the sight of the beauty and the perfection of her form. He began to examine her in detail. He considered her statuesque thighs and her delicious navel, the whiteness of which equalled that of ivory: her belly gently domed like an elegant arch: her well-formed chest on which rose majestically breasts which resembled the calyx of a flower. Her neck was like the neck of a gazelle, the opening of her mouth like a ring, and her fresh red lips were like a dripping sword. Her teeth were like pearls and her cheeks were like roses. Her eyes were black and well defined, and her brows described a graceful arc.

Bahloul began to embrace her, to suck her lips, to kiss her throat, and to move his lips over her cheeks. He nibbled her breasts, drank her sweet saliva, and bit her thighs. He continued this until she was enravished and could no longer speak or keep her eyes open. Then he kissed her vulva and she moved neither hands nor feet. He let his eyes linger lovingly on her natural parts which were like a purple-centred dome.

'Oh, temptation of mankind!' he cried, though he did not cease to kiss and bite until the impulse was keenly felt. Hamdouna redoubled her sighs and, seizing Bahloul's member, she guided it in. It was for him then to move his buttocks and for her to accompany him in their duet of love. This she did so ardently that their enjoyment was simultaneous.

Bahloul then arose and wiped his member and she her vulva; then he wished to retire, but Hamdouna said:

'Where is the robe? Are you making fun of me?'

'Oh, mistress, I shall only surrender it if you pay the price.'

'But what is your price?'

'You have had what you like and so have I. The first time was for you, the second for me, and the third shall be for the robe.'

Bahloul then took off the robe, folded it and gave it to Hamdouna who then lay down again and said:

'Do as you will!'

He at once fell on her and with a single push buried his member completely; then he set to work like a pestle, and she to shake her croup, and thus they continued until the two ejaculations arrived. Then he got up, wiped his member, abandoned the robe and went away.

Her servant said to Hamdouna:

'Oh, my mistress, is it not as I told you? Bahloul is a wicked man, and you haven't been able to best him. People make fun of him but it is he who makes fun of them. Why didn't you take my word?'

'Do not bore me with your observations. I quite expected what has happened. Bahloul is a wicked man, but he can claim admission, whether such be lawful or no, and independently of love or hate.

While they were thus talking someone knocked at the door. The servant asked who was there, and she heard Bahloul reply: 'It is I.' Hamdouna wondered what the jester wanted now, and began to feel afraid. The servant asked him what he wanted, and he replied:

'Bring me a drink of water.'

She took him some water, and, when he had drunk, he dropped the cup on the ground so that it broke. The servant closed the door, leaving Bahloul sitting on the step, and there he remained until Hamdouna's husband arrived, who said to him:

'How is it you are here, Bahloul?'

'Oh, Lord, I was passing down the street when I was seized with a great thirst. An attendant came and brought me a cup of water. The cup slipped from my hands and broke. Then our mistress Hamdouna, to make good the damage, deprived me of the robe which our master the Sultan had given me.'

'Let the robe be returned to him,' commanded the Vizier.'

At this moment Hamdouna came out of the house and her husband asked her if it was true that she had taken the golden robe in payment for the cup. Shaking with fear, Hamdouna exclaimed:

'What have you done, Bahloul?'

'I have spoken to your husband in the language of folly, speak you to him with wisdom.'

She was delighted with the trick he had played, so gave him back the robe and let him go away.

CONCERNING PRAISEWORTHY WOMEN

Know, oh Vizier (may the blessing of god be upon you!) that there are women of divers kinds, some worthy of praise, others beneath contempt.

For a woman to be relished by man she must have a fine figure well endowed with flesh. Her hair should be black, her forehead wide; her brows should have the blackness of the Ethiopian's; her eyes should be big and black with pure whites. Her cheeks must be a perfect oval; she will have an elegant nose and a graceful mouth; her lips will be vermilion, as also her tongue; her breath will be agreeable, and her neck long and shapely; her bust and hips will be wide; her breasts must be firm and fill her chest; her belly must be well-proportioned and her navel developed and sunken; her vulva should be prominent and rich in flesh from the pubes to the buttocks; the passage must be narrow, free from humidity, soft to the touch and warm; her thighs must be hard, as also her buttocks; her waist must be slender; her hands and feet will be noticeable for their elegance; her arms will be plump, and her sholders strong. If a woman possessing these qualities is seen from before, the sight is ravishing; if from behind, fatal. Viewed sitting, she is a rounded dome; lying, a downy bed; standing, she is as a flag-staff. When she walks her natural parts stand out under her clothing. She seldom speaks or laughs, and never without reason. She never leaves the house even to visit her neighbours. She has no

woman-friend. She confides in no-one, and her husband is her sole support. She accepts no gifts but from her husband or his relations. If any of his relations are in the house she does not interfere with their business. She is not treacherous and has no faults to hide. She irritates nobody. If her husband intimates that he wishes to fulfil his conjugal duty she conforms to his desires and at times anticipates them. She always helps him in his business; she is sparing with complaints and tears; she does not laugh if she sees that her husband is downcast or sad, but she shares his troubles and fondles him till they have vanished, and she has no rest until she sees him content. She gives herself to none but her husband even though her abstinence may cause her death. She hides her secret parts from sight, observes the greatest cleanliness, and hides from her husband anything which might be repugnant to him. She perfumes herself and cleans her teeth with walnut bark.

Such a wife should be cherished by all men.

CONCERNING THE GENERATIVE ACT

Know, oh Vizier (may God protect you!) that, when you desire to copulate, let it be when your stomach is free from food. Only then is coition healthful and good. But if your stomach is loaded, the result will be bad for both persons; you will be liable to an attack of apoplexy and gout, and the least of the ills likely to afflict you will be either a stoppage of the urine or a weakness of sight. Let your stomach be free from all excess of food and drink and you will have nothing to fear.

Do not unite with a woman until you have excited her with playful caresses and then the pleasure will be mutual. It is advisable therefore to amuse yourselves before you introduce your member and accomplish the act. You will excite her by kissing her cheeks, sucking her lips, and nibbling her teats. You will kiss her navel and thighs, and lay a provoking hand upon her pubes. Bite her arms; do not neglect any part of her body; clasp her tightly till she feels your love; then sigh and twine your arms and legs round hers.

When you are with a woman and you see that her eyes languish and she sighs profoundly, in a word, when she desires to copulate, let your two passions blend and your lubricity be carried to the highest point; for, so far as enjoyment is concerned, the favourable moment has arrived. The woman will then experience the supremest pleasure; you yourself will love her more and

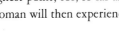

28

she will cling to you. It has been well said that: 'When you hear a woman sighing profoundly, and see her lips and ears become red and her eyes languishing, her mouth become slack and her movements slow; when she seems as if inclined for sleep and frequently yawns, know that this is the right moment for coition. If you penetrate her now her pleasure will be supreme, and you will certainly awaken the sucking power of her vagina, which yields, without any doubt, the highest pleasure for both, and is the best guarantee that love will endure.

The following precepts were given by a student of the art of love: 'Woman is like a fruit which will only yield its fragance when rubbed by the hands. Take, for example, the basil: unless

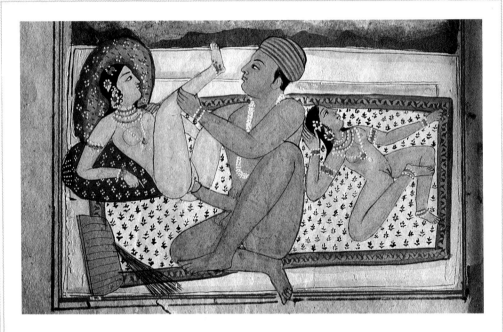

it be warmed by the fingers it emits no perfume. And do you not know that unless amber be warmed and manipulated it retains its aroma within? The same with woman: if you do not animate her with your frolics and kisses, with nibbling of her thighs and close embraces, you will not obtain what you desire; you will experience no pleasure when she shares your couch, and she will feel no affection for you.

It is related that a man, having questioned a woman as to the things most likely to inspire affection for a man, received the following answer: 'The things which develop love for the moment of coition are the playful frolics practised in advance, and the vigorous embrace at the moment of ejaculation. Believe me, kisses, nibblings, sucking of lips, close-clasping of breasts, and the drinking of passion-loaded spittle, are the things which ensure a durable affection. Acting thus, the two ejaculations occur simultaneously, and enjoyment is complete for both. Add to that, the sucker will be brought into action, and no higher pleasure can be conceived. If things do not happen so, the woman's pleasure is incomplete and, if her desires are not satisfied and her sucker wakened to action, she will feel no love for her partner; but when the sucker is in action, she will have the most violent love for her lover, even though he be the ugliest man on earth. Try then by all means to make the ejaculations simultaneous, for that is the secret of love.'

One of the cleverest men who have made a study of women relates the following feminine confidence: 'Oh, you men who seek for the love and affection of women and desire to retain them, see that you frolic before copulation. Prepare her for the enjoyment and let nothing be neglected to attain this end. Explore her with all possible activity and, while so doing, let your mind be free from all other thought. Do not let pleasure's propitious moment pass by unheeded: it occurs when you see her eyes slightly moist and her mouth partly open. Unite,

then, but never before. Therefore, oh men, when you have brought woman to the favourable condition, introduce your member; then if you take care to move in the proper manner, she will experience a pleasure which will satisfy all her desires. Do not rise yet from her breast, but let your lips wander over her cheeks, and let your sword rest in her sheath. Seek ardently to arouse her sucker, so will your work be worthily crowned. If by the favour of the All-highest you achieve success, be careful not to withdraw your member, but let it remain and drain the cup of pleasure. Give ear and listen to the sighs and cries and murmurs of the woman, for these bear witness to the violence of the pleasure you have procured her.

And when the cessation of enjoyment puts an end to your amorous frolics, take care not to rise brusquely, but withdraw your member with circumspection; stay with the woman, lying on your right side in this bed of pleasure. In this way nothing but good will result, and you will not be like those who mount a woman as a mule would, paying no attention to the principles of the art, and who withdraw and hurry away as soon as they have ejaculated. So crude a method must be avoided as it deprives the woman of all pleasure.'

To sum up, it behoves the connoisseur of copulation to omit none of my recommendations, for it is on the observance of these that woman's happiness depends.

CONCERNING ALL THAT IS FAVOURABLE
TO COITION

Know, oh Vizier, (God's mercy be with you!) that if you wish to experience an agreeable copulation, one that gives equal satisfaction and pleasure to both parties, it is necessary to frolic with the woman and excite her with nibbling, kissing, and caressing. Turn her over on the bed, sometimes on her back, sometimes on her belly, until you see by her eyes that the moment of pleasure has arrived, as I have described in the previous chapter, and, on my honour! I have not stinted the descriptions.

When, therefore, you see a woman's lips tremble and redden, and her eyes become languishing and her sighs profound, know that she desires coition; then is the time to get between her thighs and penetrate her. If you have followed my advice you will both enjoy a delightful copulation which will leave a delicious memory. Someone has said: 'If you desire to copulate, place the woman on the ground, embrace her closely and put your lips on hers; then clasp her, suck her, bite her; kiss her neck, her breasts, her belly and her flanks; strain her to you until she lies limp with desire. When you see her in this state, introduce your member. If you act thus your enjoyment will be simultaneous, and that is the secret of pleasure. But if you neglect this plan the woman will not satisfy your desires, and she herself will gain no enjoyment.'

When the act is finished and you wish to rise, do not do so suddenly, but withdraw gently from her right side and, if she has conceived, she will bear a son — if God will have it so! It has been said by some wise man (may God pardon him!) that if someone puts his hand on a pregnant woman's vulva and says: 'In the name of God! let His mercy be with His Prophet! Oh God, I pray You, in the name of the Prophet, let this be a boy,' it may happen that by the will of God and in consideration of our Lord Mohammed, (on whom be God's mercy!) the woman will bear a boy.

Do not drink rain-water immediately after coition as it tends to weaken the loins.

If you wish to repeat the act, perfume yourself with sweet odours, then approach the woman, and you will attain a happy result.

It is advisable to rest after coition and not indulge in any violent exercise.

CONCERNING THE DIFFERENT
POSTURES FOR COITION

The ways of uniting with a woman are numerous and varied, and the time has arrived when you should learn the different postures. God has said: 'Woman is your field, go to your field with a will!' (Koran).

According to your taste you may choose the posture which pleases you most, provided always that intercourse takes place through the appointed organ: the vulva.

First posture Lay the woman on her back and raise her thighs; then, getting between her legs,

introduce your member. Gripping the ground with your toes, you will be able to move in a suitable manner. This posture is a good one for those who have long members.

Second posture If your member is short, lay the woman on her back and raise her legs in the air so that her toes touch her ears. Her buttocks being thus raised, the vulva is thrown forward. Now introduce your member.

Third posture Lay the woman on the ground and get between her thighs; then, putting one of her legs on your shoulder and the other under your arm, penetrate her.

Fourth posture Stretch the woman on the ground and put her legs on your shoulders; in that position your member will be exactly opposite her vulva which will be lifted off the ground. That is the moment for introducing your member.

Fifth posture Let the woman lie on her side on the ground; then, lying down yourself and getting between her thighs, introduce your member. This posture is apt to give rise to rheumatic or sciatic pains.

Sixth posture Let the woman rest on her knees and elbows in the position for prayer. In this posture the vulva stands out behind. Attack her thus.

Seventh posture Lay the woman on her side, and then you yourself sitting on your heels will place her top leg on your nearest shoulder and her other leg aginst your thighs. She will keep on her side and you will be between her legs. Introduce your member and move her backwards and forwards with your hands.

Eighth posture Lay the woman on her back and kneel astride her.

Ninth posture Place the woman so that she rests, either face forward or the reverse, against a slightly raised platform, her feet remaining on the ground and her body projecting in front. She will thus present her vulva to your member which you will introduce.

Tenth posture Place the woman on a rather low divan and let her grasp the woodwork with her hands; then, placing her legs on your hips and telling her to grip your body with them, you will introduce your member, at the same time grasping the divan. When you begin to work, let your movements keep time.

Eleventh posture Lay the woman on her back and let her buttocks be raised by a cushion placed under them. Let her put the soles of her feet together: now get between her thighs.

There are other postures besides the preceding in use in India. It is well that you should know that the Hindus have greatly multiplied the ways of possessing a woman and have carried their investigations in this matter much farther than the Arabs.

Among other postures and variations are the following:

35

The closure Lay the woman on her back and raise her buttocks with a cushion; then get between her legs, keeping your toes on the floor, and force her thighs against her chest. Now pass your hands under her arms to clasp her to you, or tightly grip her shoulders. That done, introduce your member and draw her towards you at the moment of ejaculation. This posture is painful for the woman, for, with her thighs pressed on her chest and her buttocks raised with the cushion, the walls of the vagina are forced together, and, as a consequence — the uterus being pushed forward — there is not enough room for the penis which can only be inserted with difficulty, and which impinges on the womb. This posture should only be used when the penis is short and soft.

The frog's posture Place the woman on her back and raise her thighs till her heels are close to her buttocks. Now seat yourself in front of her vulva and introduce your member; then put her knees under your armpits and, grasping the upper part of her arms, draw her to you at the propitious moment.

The clasping of hands and feet Lay the woman on her back, then sit on your heels between her thighs and grip the floor with your toes; she will now put her legs round your body and you will put your arms about her neck.

The raised legs posture While the woman is lying on her back take hold of her legs and, holding them close together, raise them until her soles point to the ceiling; then clasping her between your thighs, introduce your member, taking care at the same time not to let her legs fall.

The goat's posture Let the woman lie on her side and stretch out the bottom leg. Crouch down between her thighs, lift her top leg and introduce your member. Hold her by the arms or shoulders.

The Archimedean screw While the man is lying on his back the woman sits on his member, keeping her face towards his. She then places her hands on the bed, at the same time keeping her belly off his; she now moves up and down and, if the man is light in weight, he may move as well. If the woman wishes to kiss the man she need only lay her arms on the bed.

The stab with a lance Suspend the woman face upwards from the ceiling by means of four cords attached to her hands and feet and another supporting the middle of her body. Her position should be such that her vulva is now opposite your member, you standing up. Introduce your member and then begin to swing her, first away from you, then towards you. You thus alternately introduce and withdraw your member, and so you continue until you ejaculate.

The hanging posture The woman lies face downwards, and the man fixes cords to her hands and feet and raises her by means of a pulley fixed to the ceiling. He then lies under her, holds the other end of the rope in his hand, and lets her down so that he can penetrate her. He raises and lowers her until he ejaculates.

The summersault The woman should let her trousers fall to her ankles so that they are like fetters. She then bends down till her head is in her trousers, when the man, seizing her legs, pulls her over onto her back. He then kneels down and penetrates her. It is said that there are women, who, when lying on their back, can put their feet under their head without the help of their hands or trousers.

The ostrich's tail Lay the woman on the ground and kneel at her feet; then raise her legs and place them round your neck so that only her head and shoulders remain on the ground. Now penetrate her.

Putting on the sock The woman being on her back, you sit between her legs and place your member between the lips of her vulva which you grasp with the thumb and first finger. You then move so that the part of your member which is in contact with the woman is subjected to rubbing, and continue so until her vulva is moist with the liquid which escapes from your penis. Having thus given her a foretaste of pleasure, you penetrate her completely.

The mutual view of the buttocks The man lies on his back, and the woman, turning her back to him, sits on his member. He now clasps her body with his legs and she leans over until her hands touch the floor. Thus supported she has a view of his buttocks, and he of hers, and she is able to move conveniently.

Drawing the bow Let the woman lie on her side, and the man, also on his side, get between her legs so that his face is turned towards her back; now, placing his hands on her shoulders, he introduces his member. The woman then grasps the man's feet and draws them towards her; she forms thus, with the man's body, a bow to which she is the arrow.

Reciprocating motion The man, seated on the ground, brings the soles of his feet together, at the same time lowering his thighs. The woman then sits on his feet and clasps his body with her legs and his neck with her arms. The man then grasps the woman's legs, and, moving his feet towards his body, carries the woman within reach of his member, which he introduces. By a movement of his feet he now moves her backwards and forwards. The woman should take care to facilitate this movement by not pressing too heavily. If the man fears that his member will be drawn right out, he must grasp the woman round the body and be satisfied with such movement as he can give with his feet.

Pounding the spot The man sits down and stretches out his legs, and the woman sits on his thighs and crosses her legs behind his back. She places her vulva opposite his penis and lends a guiding hand. She then puts her arms round his neck, and he puts his round her waist and raises and lowers her on his member, in which movement she assists.

Coition from behind The woman lies face downwards and raises her buttocks with a cushion; the man lies on her back and introduces his member while she slips her arms through his elbows.

Belly to belly The man and the woman stand face to face, the latter with her feet slightly apart,

the man's feet being between. Both now advance their feet. The man should now place one foot in advance of the other, and each should clasp the other round the loins. The man then penetrates and both move in the manner explained later on. (See first movement.)

The sheep's posture The woman kneels down and puts her fore-arms on the ground; the man kneels down behind her and slips his penis in her vulva which she makes stand out as much as possible. His hands should be placed on her shoulders.

The camel's hump The woman, who is standing, bends forward till her fingers touch the floor; the man gets behind and copulates, at the same time grasping her thighs. If the man withdraws while the woman is still bending down, the vagina emits a sound like the bleating of a calf, and for that reason women object to the posture.

Driving in the peg While facing each other, the woman, hanging with her arms round the man's neck, raises her legs and with them clasps him round the waist, resting her feet against a wall. The man now introduces his member, and the woman is then as if hanging on a peg.

The fusion of love The woman lies on her right side and you on your left; stretch your bottom leg straight down and raise your other leg, letting it rest on the woman's side. Now pull the woman's top leg onto your body and then introduce your member. The woman may help if she likes, to make the necessary movements.

Coition by violence The man goes up behind the woman and takes her by surprise. He thrusts his hands below her armpits and onto the back of her neck, at the same time forcing her head down. If she is not wearing trousers he will try to lift her dress with his knees, and preventing her from moving her legs by pressing against them so that she cannot turn and so prevent the introduction of his member. But, if she is strong and wearing trousers, he will be obliged to hold both her hands with one of his, and, with the other, pull her garment down.

Inversion The man lies on his back and the woman lies on him. She grasps his thighs and draws them towards her, thus bringing his member into prominence. Having guided it in, she puts her hands on the bed, one on each side of the man's buttocks. It is necessary for her feet to be raised on a cushion to allow for the slope of the penis. The woman moves.

This posture may be varied by the woman sitting on her heels between the man's legs.

Riding the member The man lies down and places a cushion under his shoulders, taking care that his buttocks remain on the floor. Thus placed, he raises his legs till his knees are close to his face. The woman then sits on his member. She does not lie down, but sits astride, as though on a saddle formed by the man's legs and chest. By bending her knees she can now move upwards and downwards; or, she may put her knees on the floor, in which case the man moves her with his thighs while she grasps his shoulders.

The jointer The man and the woman sit down facing each other; the woman then puts her right thigh on the man's left thigh, and he puts his right thigh on her left one. The woman guides his member into her vagina and grasps the man's arms while he grasps hers. They now indulge in a see-saw motion, leaning backwards and forwards alternately, taking care that their movements are well-timed.

The stay-at-home The woman lies on her back, and the man, with cushions under his hands, lies on her. When the introduction has taken place the woman raises her buttocks as far as possible from the bed, and the man accompanies her in the movement, taking care that his member is not withdrawn. The woman then drops her buttocks with short sharp jerks, and, although the two are not clasped together, the man should keep quite close to the woman. They continue this movement, but it is necessary that the man be light and the bed soft; otherwise pain will be caused.

The blacksmith's posture The woman lies on her back with a cushion under her buttocks. She now draws her knees onto her chest so that her vulva stands out like a sieve; she then guides in the member. The man now performs for a moment or two the conventional movements. He then withdraws his member and slips it between the women's thighs in imitation of the blacksmith who draws the hot iron from the fire and plunges it into cold water.

The seductive posture The woman lies on her back and the man crouches between her legs which he then puts under his arms or on his shoulders. He may hold her by the waist or the arms.

The preceding descriptions furnish a greater number of postures than can generally be made

use of; but the large number will enable those who experience any difficulty in practising some of them to find which suit them the best and give them most pleasure.

I have not thought it necessary to mention those postures which appeared to me impossible of accomplishment and, if anyone should think the number given is too small, he has nothing to do but invent more.

It is incontestable that the Hindus have surmounted enormous difficulties in postures for coition; the following is an example:

The woman lies on her back and the man sits astride her chest, facing towards her feet. He now bends forward and raises her thighs till her vulva is opposite his member which he then introduces.

As you can see, this posture is difficult to execute and very tiring. I think it is only realizable in thought or design.

It is related that there are women who, during coition, can raise one of their legs in the air and balance a lighted lamp on the sole of their foot, without spilling the oil or extinguishing the lamp. Intercourse is not interfered with by this action which demands, however, great skill.

Nevertheless, the things to be sought for most in copulation, those which give the greatest pleasure, are the embraces, the kisses, and the sucking of each other's lips. These differentiate man from the animals. No-one is insensible to the pleasures which arise from difference of sex, and man's highest pleasure is copulation.

When a man's love is carried to its highest pitch, all the pleasures of coition become easy for

him, and he satisfies them by embracing and kissing. There is the real source of happiness for both.

It is advisable that the connoisseur of copulation should try all the postures so that he may know which gives pleasure to the woman. He will then adopt that for preference and will have the satisfaction of retaining the woman's affection. By universal consent, the fifteenth posture (pounding on the spot) gives most satisfaction.

It is related that a man had a mistress of incomparable beauty, grace, and perfection. He was in the habit of copulating with her in the ordinary way to the exclusion of any other. The woman experienced none of the pleasure which should accompany the act, and was always ill-tempered afterwards. The man told his trouble to an old woman, who said: 'Try different methods of copulating with your mistress and see which gives her most pleasure. When you have found it, never use another, and she will love you without bounds.'

So the man tried various postures, and when he came to the one call Pounding on the Spot, he saw that the woman's pleasure was intense, and felt his member powerfully seized. The woman exclaimed, while biting his lips: 'That's the proper way to make love!'

These demonstrations proved to the lover that his mistress experienced the greatest pleasure from this posture, so he never used another.

Try, then, the different postures, for every woman prefers the one which gives her the greatest pleasure; but the majority show a marked predilection for the one before-mentioned, for, in practising it, belly is pressed against belly; and mouth on mouth, and rarely does the sucker fail to act.

It remains now for me to speak of the different movements used in copulation.
First movement. **The bucket in the well** The man and woman embrace closely after penetration, then the man moves once and slightly draws back; the woman now moves and withdraws in her turn, and so on alternately. They should take care to place their hands and feet against each others and imitate, as well as they can, the descent of a bucket in a well.
Second movement. **The mutual shock** Both draw away after the introduction, taking care that the member is not entirely withdrawn; they then come together smartly and closely embrace. They continue thus.
Third movement. **Going shares** The man moves in the usual manner, then stops; the woman,

47

keeping the member in place, moves once, then stops. The man now recommences, and so they continue till they ejaculate.

Fourth movement. **Love's tailor** The man partly penetrates and moves with a rubbing motion; then, with a single stroke, he enters completely. Such is the action of a tailor who, after having inserted his needle, draw it through with a single pull. This movement is only suitable for those who can control their ejaculation.

Fifth movement. **The tooth-pick** The man introduces his member and explores the vagina from top to bottom and on all sides. This movement requires a vigorous instrument.

Sixth movement. **Love's bond** The man penetrates completely so that his body is perfectly close to the woman's. He should now move energetically, taking care that not the smallest portion is withdrawn from the vulva.

This is the best movement of all, and it is particularly suitable for the fifteenth posture. Women prefer it to the exclusion of all others as it procures them the greatest pleasure, and allows the vagina to clasp the penis. Tribads use no other movement, and it can be recommended to all who suffer from a premature ejaculation.

Any posture is unsatisfactory if kissing is impossible; pleasure will be incomplete, for a kiss is one of the most potent stimulants that a man or woman can indulge in. For woman it is particularly so, especially if she is alone and sheltered from indiscreet regards.

It is claimed by some that kissing is an integral part of copulation.

The most delightful kiss is that which is planted on moist ardent lips, and accompanied with suction of the lips and tongue, so that the emission of a sweet intoxicating saliva is produced. It

is for the man to procure this emission from the woman by gently nibbling her lips and tongue till she secretes a particular saliva, sweet, exquisite, more agreeable than honey mixed with pure water, and which does not mix with her ordinary saliva. This gives the man a shivering sensation throughout his whole body, and is more intoxicating than strong wine.

A kiss should be sonorous. Its sound, light and prolonged, takes its rise between the tongue and the moist edge of the palate. It is produced by a movement of the tongue in the mouth and a displacement of the saliva provoked by suction.

A kiss given on the outside of the lips and accompanied with a sound like that made when calling a cat, gives no pleasure whatever. Such a kiss is only meant for children, or the hands. The kiss which I have described above, and which belongs to copulation provokes a delicious voluptuousness. It is for you to learn the difference.

Know that all the kisses and caresses mentioned above are useless if unaccompanied by the introduction of the penis. You should therefore abstain if not able to copulate, or otherwise you light a fire which only a sterile separation can quench. Passion which inflames resembles a fire, and as only water can extinguish this, so only can semen extinguish the fires of love. Woman is no more satisfied than man with caresses unfollowed by copulation.

It is related that Dahama ben Mesejel complained before the governor of the province of Yahama that her husband, El Ajaje, was impotent and neither cohabited with her nor approached her. Her father, who assisted her in the case, was blamed by the people of Yamama for this, and they asked him if he was not ashamed to demand coition for his daughter.

'I want her to have some children,' replied he; 'if she loses them, God will hold her to account; if she keeps them, they will be useful.'

Dahama presented her case in these words to the emir:
'Here is my husband; up to now he has left me intact.'

'You are perhaps unwilling,' objected the emir.

'On the contrary, I willingly lie down and open my legs.'

'Oh emir, she lies! If I want to possess her I have to fight hard,' exclaimed her husband.

'I will give you a year in which to prove the falsity of the allegation,' replied the emir to him. This he did, however, out of sympathy for the man.

El Ajaje then withdrew.

As soon as he got back home he took his wife in his arms and began to caress her and kiss her on the mouth; but that was the limit of his efforts, for he could give no proof of his virility. Dahama said to him: 'Cease your caresses and embraces; they do not suffice for love. What I need is a strong and rigid member whose sperm will flood my womb.'

In despair, Ajaje took her back to her family and repudiated her that very night.

Know then that if a woman is to be satisfied, kisses without coition will not suffice. Her sole delight is in the penis, and she gives her love to the man who can use it well, however disagreeable and deformed he is.

It is related that Moussa ben Mesab went one day to the house of a lady who owned a female slave, a beautiful singer, to see if he could buy her. Now this lady was a great beauty and very rich. When he entered the house he noticed a man, still young but very deformed, who was giving orders. He enquired of the lady who the man was, and she replied:
'That is my husband, and I would willingly die for him.'

'You are reduced to a hard slavery, and I pity you; but we belong to God and shall return to Him! Still, what a calamity that such incomparable beauty and such a figure should belong to that man!'

'Oh son, if he did to you behind what he does to me in front, you would sell all your goods and even your patrimony. You would then think him handsome, and his ugliness would change to perfection.'

'May God preserve him for you!' exclaimed Moussa.

CONCERNING THE DIVERS NAMES
OF THE VIRILE MEMBER

Know, oh Vizier (God grant you mercy!), that the virile member had many names, among which are the following:

> The virile member · Generative organ ·
> Smith's bellows · Pigeon · Jingler · Untameable ·
> Liberator · Creeper · Exciter · Deceiver · Sleeper ·
> Pathmaker · Tailor · Quencher · Twister · Knocker ·
> Swimmer · Enterer · Withdrawer · One-eyed ·
> Bald-head · One with an eye · Stumbler ·
> Funny-head · One with a neck · Hairy one ·
> Shameless one · Bashful one · Weeper · Mover ·
> Annexer · Spitter · Splasher · Breaker ·
> Seeker · Rubber · Flabby one · Searcher · Discoverer.

The first two names present no difficulty.

The smith's bellows It has received this name because of its alternative inflation and deflation.

The pigeon It is so called because, after having been swollen and at the moment when it is returning to its state of repose, it resembles a pigeon settling on its eggs.

The jingler It is so called on account of the noise it makes each time it enters or leaves the vulva.

The untameable It has received this name because, when it is swollen and erect, it starts to move its head, looking for the entrance to the vagina, which, when found, it brusquely and insolently enters.

The liberator So named because, when entering the vulva of a divorced woman, it frees her from the prohibition of remarrying her former husband.

The creeper This name has been given to the penis because, when it gets between a woman's thighs and sees a plump vulva, it starts to creep on her legs and pubis, then, approaching the entrance, it continues to creep until it has taken possession. When comfortably installed it penetrates completely and ejaculates.

The exciter It has received this name because it irritates the vulva with its repeated entrances and exits.

The deceiver It gets this name from its tricks and ruses. When it desires coition, it says: 'If God gives me the chance of meeting with a vulva, I will never quit it!' but, when it finds one, it is soon satisfied, its presumption becomes apparent and it throws a despairing look at the vulva, for it bragged that once inside it would never come out. At the approach of a woman it draws itself up and seems to say to the vulva: 'Today, oh my soul, I will quench my desires with you!', and the vulva, seeing it erect and stiff, is surprised at its size and seems to reply: 'Whoever could accommodate such a member?' Its only reply is to place its head at the door of the vulva, force open the lips and sink right in. When it starts to move the vulva makes fun of it and says: 'What a deceptive movement!' for he is no sooner in than out. The two testicles seem to say: 'Our friend is dead; he has succumbed after his pleasure, the quenching of his passion and the ejaculation of his sperm!' He then withdraws precipitately from the vulva and tries to hold up his head again, but he falls flabby and inert. The testicles repeat: 'Our brother is dead . . . our brother is dead!' He protests, saying: 'Nothing of the kind!' But the vulva exclaims: 'Why do you withdraw? Oh, liar, you said that when once you were in you would never come out.'

The sleeper This name is due to its deceptive appearance. When it enters in erection it lenghtens and stiffens to such a pitch that you would never think it would soften again, but, when it leaves the vulva after slaking its passion, it falls asleep.

The pathmaker It has this name because, when it meets a vulva which will not let it enter at once, it makes a passage with its head, breaking and tearing all like a ruttish beast.

The tailor It gets this name from the fact that it does not enter the vulva until after it has manoeuvred at the entrance, like a needle in the hand of a tailor.

The quencher This name is given to a thick strong member which is slow to ejaculate. Such a member fully satisfies woman's amorous desires because, after having raised them to the highest pitch, it quenches them better than any other. When it wishes to enter a vulva and, on arriving at the entrance, finds it closed, it laments, pleads, and makes promises backed by pledges: 'Oh, dear friend, let me enter . . . I will not stay long'; but, when it has gained its cause, it breaks its word by prolonging its stay, and not withdrawing until after it has ejaculated and exhausted its ardour by dint of moving in and out, up and down, and right and left. The vulva demands: 'What about your promise, oh liar? You said you would only stay a moment! But he replies: 'Oh, I shall not withdraw until I have met your womb, but I promise to do so then.' At these words the vulva is overcome with pity, it wakes the sucker which grips the member by the head and satisfies it completely.

The twister This name was given to it because it arrives at the vulva as if on urgent business. It knocks at the door, twists and turns about in a shameless manner, pushing its investigations to right and left, before and behind, then suddenly penetrating to the bottom of the vagina to ejaculate.

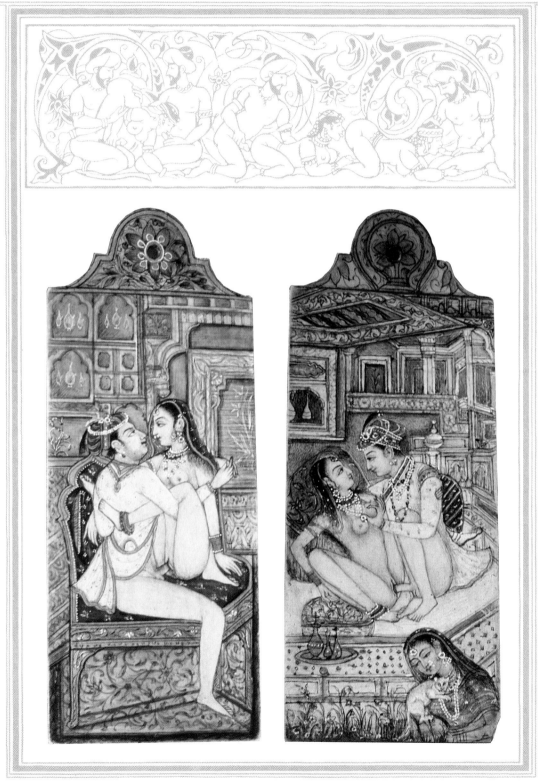

The knocker It is thus named because, when it arrives at the door of the vulva, it gives a light knock; if the vulva replies and opens the door, it enters; but, if it gets no reply, it knocks again until successful. By knocking at the door we refer to the rubbing of the penis on the vulva until it becomes moist. The production of this moisture is what is called opening the door.

The swimmer This is the one which, when it enters the vagina, does not remain in one place but turns to the right and left, before and behind, but principally in the middle, and swims about in the sperm which it ejects and the fluid secreted by the woman as if, fearing to be drowned, it struggles to save its life.

The enterer This merits its name because, when it arrives at the door of the vulva, this latter says: 'What is your wish?' and replies: 'I wish to enter.' The vulva replies: 'That is impossible . . . I cannot receive you on account of your size.' The enterer then asks to be allowed to introduce its head, promising not to penetrate completely; it approaches the vulva, rubs its head two or three times between the lips until it has provoked the secretion, then, when the vulva is well lubricated, it takes a sudden plunge and buries itself completely.

The withdrawer So called because, when it approaches a vulva which has been deprived for a long time of coitus and which it wishes to enter, the vulva will say (influenced by the violence of its amorous desire): 'Yes, but on one condition . . . that, if you enter, you will not withdraw until you have ejaculated so many times!' The member replies: 'I promise not to withdraw until I have done it three times more than you ask.' Once entered, the intensity of the vulva's heat activates the enjoyment; it moves up and down, seeking the perfect pleasure which this movement procures by the alternate rubbings against the vulva and the womb. When the ejaculation takes place the member seeks to withdraw, which makes the vulva say: 'Oh, liar, why do you withdraw? You ought to be called the lying withdrawer.'

The one-eyed The force of this name is obvious.

The bald-head As above.

The one with an eye It has this name because its solitary eye presents this peculiarity, that it has neither pupils nor lashes.

The stumbler It has been so called because, when it wishes to enter the vulva and not seeing the door, it bumps above and below and continues so as if it were stumbling against a stone on the road, until the lips of the vulva are lubricated and it can enter. The vulva then asks: 'What made you stumble so?' 'Oh, my friend, there was a stone in my way,' it replies.

The funny-head It has this name because its head is different from all others.

The one with a neck It is he whose neck is short and thick and big behind. Its head is skinned and the pubic hair is stubborn.

The hairy one This needs no explanation.

The shameless one It has received this name because, from the minute it gets stiff and long, it cares for nobody. It unblushingly lifts its master's raiment, caring nought for the shame he feels. It acts in the same shameless way with woman. It will lift her clothes and expose her thighs. Its master may feel shame at this conduct, but, as for itself, its stiffness and ardour go on increasing.

The bashful one This member, met with in some individuals, feels shame and becomes bashful when in the presence of an unknown vulva, and it is only after a time that it raises its head. Sometimes its trouble is so great that it remains quite impotent, especially if a stranger is near.

The weeper So called because of the many tears it sheds. As soon as it stands, it begins to weep; if it sees a pretty face, it weeps; if it touches a woman, it weeps. It even at times weeps tears of remembrance.

The mover So called because, as soon as it enters the vulva, it moves about till its ardour is quenched.

The annexer This gets its name because, when it enters the vulva, it starts to move, but, at the same time, clings closely hair to hair and even tries to force the testicles in.

The spitter It has received this name because, at the approach of the vulva or at its aspect, or even simply at its memory, or when its master touches a woman, plays with her or kisses her, its saliva begins to flow; this saliva is particularly abundant after a long abstinence and will sometimes soak the clothing. This member is very common and few are the men not so endowed.

The liquid thus poured out is known as the medi. A discharge may be caused by lascivious thoughts. It is so abundant with some men that it fills the vulva, so much so that many think it derives from the woman.

The splasher So called because it makes a splashing noise when it enters the vulva.

The breaker This is the vigorous member which gets long and stiff like a rod or a bone. It easily breaks through a maidenhead.

The seeker This name was given because, when it is in the vulva, it starts to move about as if it were looking for something. It is looking for the womb, and it has no peace till it finds it.

The rubber It gets this name because it does not enter the vagina until it has rubbed against the vulva several times. It is often counfounded with the following.

The flabby one The one which can never penetrate because it is too soft and so must be content with rubbing against the vulva until it ejaculates. It gives no pleasure to a woman for it only enflames her passions and cannot quench them.

The searcher So called because it penetrates into unusual places, takes particulars of the state of vulvas, and knows how to distinguish their good and bad qualities.

The discoverer It has been so called because, when it gets stiff and holds up its head, it lifts the

clothes which hide it and so betrays its master by uncovering his nudity; nor does it fear to expose the vulvas which are unknown to it by shamelessly lifting the women's garments. It is quite inaccessible to any feeling of shame and has no respect for anyone. Nothing relative to coition is unknown to it. It has a profound knowledge of the humidity, freshness, dryness, narrowness, or heat of vulvas, the insides of which are well-known to it. There are some vulvas which are externally perfect, plump and good-looking, while their interior is far from satisfactory. They give no pleasure because of their excessive moisture or their lack of warmth. It is because this member sets out to find all that can add to the pleasure of coition that it has received its name.

Such are the principal names which have been given to the virile member, corresponding to its distinguishing qualities. It is lawful for those who find the list insufficient to look for others, but I limit myself there as the names given will satisfy most of my readers.

CONCERNING THE FEMALE ORGANS

The following are the usual names:-

The passage · Vulva · Libidinous · Primitive ·
Starling · Crack · Crested One · Snub-nosed ·
Hedgehog · Taciturn · Squeezer · Importunate ·
Sprinkler · Desirer · Beauty · Sweller · High-brow ·
Spreader · Giant · Glutton · Bottomless pit ·
Two-lipped one · Camel's hump · Sieve ·
Mover · Annexer · Accommodator · Helper ·
Arch · Extender · Duellist · Ever-ready ·
Fleer · Resigned · Wet one · Barricaded one ·
Abyss · Biter · Sucker · Wasp ·
Warmer · Delicious one.

The passage It has received this name (el feuj) because it opens and closes like the vulva of a mare in heat.

The vulva Such an organ is plump and outstanding in its full length; the lips are long, the opening large, the edges apart and perfectly symmetrical, and the middle prominent; it is soft, seductive, and perfect in all its details. It is, without fear of contradiction, the most agreeable and the best of all. May God grant us the use of such a vulva! Amen! It is warm, narrow and dry to such a degree that one would think fire would dart from it. Its form is graceful, its odour suave; its whiteness throws the carmine centre into relief. In a word, it is perfect.

The libidinous A name given to a virgin's vulva.

The primitive This name is applicable to any vulva.

The starling Applied to a brunette's vulva.

The crack It is like a crack in a wall, and is devoid of flesh.

The crested one This is provided with a comb like a cock's which stands up at the moment of pleasure.

The snub-nosed This has thin lips and a tiny tongue.

The hedgehog This is where the skin is harsh and the hair coarse.

The taciturn This is the one which is sparing in words. Should a member penetrate a hundred times a day it would say nothing but would be content to look on.

The squeezer So called because of its squeezing action on the member. Immediately after penetration it starts to squeeze the member and draws it in with such gusto that were it possible, it would absorb the testicles too.

The importunate This is the vulva which will spare no member. If one spend a hundred nights with it and penetrated a hundred times a night, it would neither be tired nor satisfied, but would rather ask for more. With it, the roles are inverted: the member is the defender, and it the petitioner. However, it is very rare, being only found in those women who are all flame and fire.

The sprinkler During urination this makes a loud rustling noise.

The desirer This is only met with in a few women; in some it is a natural gift, in others it is the result of prolonged abstinence. Its distinguishing feature is that it seeks out the member, and when it has found it, it refuses to release it until its fire is quenched.

The beauty This name is given to the white plump vulva which is rounded like a dome. The eye cannot quit it, and no member can withstand it.

The sweller So called because, when a member arrives at the entrance, it is caused to swell and stand up at once. It procures enormous satisfaction for its owner, and, at the moment of enjoyment, it winks.

The high-brow This is surmounted by a pubis which resembles a stately forehead.

The spreader So called because, at the approach of the member, it appears to be closed and impenetrable to such an extent that it would seem impossible to insert the little finger; but, when a member rubs it with its head, it widens considerably.

The giant This is as long as it is wide, that is, it is developed in both directions, from side to side and from the pubis to the perineum. It is the most beautiful that the eye may ever behold. May God in His goodness never deprive us of such a sight!

The glutton This is the one with a wide throat. If it has been deprived of coition for a certain time and a member should then approach it, it will swallow it whole, as a hungry man will throw himself on to food and try to swallow it without chewing.

The bottomless pit Applied to the vagina which is prolonged indefinitely. It necessitates the use of a very long member, no other being able to satisfy its desires.

The two-lipped one This is applied to the vulva of an exceedingly stout woman.

The camel's hump This is crowned by a mons veneris which stands out like a camel's hump and which stretches between the thighs like a calf's head. God grant that we may enjoy such a vulva! Amen!

The sieve When this vulva receives a member it starts to move up and down, right and left, backwards and forwards, until complete satisfaction.

The mover When this has received the member it moves violently and without interruption until the penis reaches the womb. It takes no rest until the operation is completely terminated.

The annexer That vagina is so called, which when it has received a member, clings round it as closely as possible, so that, if it could, it would draw in the testicles.

The accommodator This name is applied to the vagina of the woman who has felt for some time an ardent desire for coition. In its satisfaction at seeing a member, it aids it in its reciprocating movement; it eagerly offers the womb, and it could offer nothing more welcome. When the member wishes to visit any particular part it lends itself graciously to the task, so that no nook is left unvisited.

When enjoyment arrives and the member wishes to ejaculate, it clasps its head and presents the womb. It then vigorously sucks the member, using all its powers to extract the sperm destined to flow into the expectant womb. And, certainly, pleasure is incomplete for the woman possessing such a vagina if the flood of semen is not poured into the womb.

The helper This vulva is so called because it helps the member to enter and withdraw or to move up and down. By this help the ejaculation is easy and enjoyment complete. Even he who is ordinarily slow to ejaculate is vanquished by this vulva.

The arch This is a large-sized vulva.

The extender This name suits only a few vulvas. The one in question extends from the pubis to the anus. It lengthens when the woman is lying or standing, and shortens when she sits, differing thereby from the round form. It resembles a magnificent cucumber stretched between the thighs. It can sometimes be seen through light clothing when the woman leans backwards.

The duellist The vulva which, once the member is in, moves with it for fear it should be withdrawn before enjoyment is complete. It feels no pleasure unless the sucker is roused so that the member can be closely clasped. Certain vulvas, animated with a violent desire for coition, either natural or as the result of prolonged continence, move forward with open mouth to meet the member like a hungry child towards its mother's breast. It is thus that this vulva moves at the approach of a member, and they then resemble two skilful duellists: as the one precipitates itself on its adversary, this latter feints to frustrate the attack. The member may be likened to a sword and the vulva to a shield. The one which ejaculates first is the vanquished, and truly it is final combat! So would I fight until my death!

The ever-ready This name is given to the vagina of a woman passionately fond of the virile member. It is the one which, far from being intimidated by a hard and stiff penis, treats it with contempt and demands one harder.

It is also the one which is neither frightened nor ashamed when someone raises the clothes which cover it; on the contrary, it gives the member the warmest welcome, lets it rest on the dome and, not content with giving it a seat on the pubis, puts it inside and buries it so completely that the testicles cry: 'Oh, what a misfortune! Our brother has disappeared. He has

plunged boldly into this gulf and we fear greatly for him. He must be the bravest of the brave to dash like that into a cavern!' The vagina, hearing their cries and wishing to allay their fears as to the disappearance of their brother, exclaims: 'Have no fear for him, he is still alive and hears your cries.' Then they reply: 'If what you say is true, let him come out that we may see him.' 'I shall not let him come out alive,' says the vulva. The testicles then ask what crime he has committed that he must be put to death — would not prision or the bastinado suffice? The vulva replies: 'By the existence of Him Who created Heaven, he shall only come out dead!' . . . then, addressing the member, it says: 'Do you hear your brothers' words? Make haste and show yourself to them for your absence afflicts them.' As soon as it has ejaculated, the member, reduced to nothing, appears to them, but they refuse to recognize it, saying: 'Who are you, oh flabby phantom?' 'I am your brother, and I was ill,' it replies; 'did you not see what state I was in before I entered? I called on all the doctors to consult them, but what a doctor I found there! He has treated my complaint and cured me without the need of examining me.' The testicles reply: 'Oh brother, we suffer the same as you, for we are one with you. Why did not God wish us to follow a treatment?' With that, the semen flows into them and augments their volume. Wishing to be treated for their illness, they say: 'Oh dear friend, make haste and take us to the doctor that he may treat us. He will know what to do, for he understands all diseases.'

The fleer It is the organ of most virgins who, not yet acquainted with the member and seeing it approach, do all they can to keep it away when it insinuates itself between their thighs to force a way in.

The resigned The one which, having received the member, patiently endures any movement it

may like to make. It is also the one which can resignedly bear the longest and most violent copulations. The hundredth time finds it still resigned and, far from complaining, it gives thanks to God. It is equally resigned when visited by several different members in succession. It is generally found in women of ardent temperament; if they had their way the man would never withdraw.

The wet one This speaks for itself. Excessive secretion militates against enjoyment.

The barricaded one This is rarely met with. The fault which characterizes it is sometimes the result of circumcision badly performed.

The abyss The one which is always gaping and whose end is out of sight and reach.

The biter The one which, when the member has penetrated, burns with such passion that it opens and shuts on the member. Especially at the moment of ejaculation the man feels his member seized by the sucker which draws like a magnet and exhausts it of its sperm. If God in his power has decreed that the woman shall conceive, the sperm is concentrated in the woman, but, if not, it is expelled.

The sucker This is the vagina which, dominated by amorous ardour resulting from continence or frequent and voluptuous caresses, grasps the member and sucks it with a strength capable of draining its sperm, acting thus as a child who sucks its mother.

The wasp This vulva is known by the strength and hardness of the pubic hair. When the member approaches it gets stung as by a wasp.

The warmer This is one of the most praiseworthy of vulvas. The pleasure of coition is measured by the degree of heat set up.

The delicious one It is reputed to procure an unequalled pleasure, only comparable to that

experienced by wild beasts and birds of prey, and for which they will fight to the death. And if it is so with animals, what must it be with man! Wars have no other cause but the search for the volupty which this vulva procures, and which is the supreme pleasure of life. It is a foretaste of the joys which await us in paradise, and only surpassed by the sight of God Himself.

It would be possible to find other names applicable to the female organs, but the number given strikes me as sufficient.

CONCERNING THE THINGS WHICH MAKE THE GENERATIVE ACT ENJOYABLE

Know, oh Vizier (God grant you His mercy!), that the things which tend to develop a passion for coition are six in number: an ardent love, an abundance of sperm, the propinquity of the person loved, beauty of face, a suitable diet, and contact.

The extreme pleasure which has its source in an impetuous and abundant ejaculation depends on one circumstance; it is imperative that the vagina be capable of suction. It then clings to the member and sucks out the semen by an irresistible attraction which is only comparable to that of a magnet. Once the member is grasped by the sucker, the man can no longer prevent the emission of semen, and the member is tightly held until it is completely drained. However, if the man ejaculates before arousing the sucker, he derives but little pleasure from the act.

Know that there are eight things which favour coition: health, freedom from worry, absence of preoccupation, a gay disposition, a generous diet, wealth, and variety in the features and complexion of the woman.

ON THE IMPORTANCE OF VIGOUR IN THE MAN (MAY GOD GRANT IT!)

The Story of Joaidi

It is related (and God penetrates the most hidden thing, and is all wise!) that, once upon a time, before the reign of the Calif Haroun al Rashid, there lived a jester who was the amusement of the women, old men and children. His name was Joaidi. He enjoyed the favours of many women and was welcomed by all. He was also well treated by the princes, viziers, and cadis, and everybody petted him. Now Joaidi has left the following tale:

I was in love with a very beautiful woman who was endowed with all imaginable graces. She had rosy cheeks, a shiny forehead, lips like coral, teeth like pearls, and breasts like pomegranates. Her mouth was like the setting of a gem; her big eyes had a sleepy languor, and her speech was of sugary sweetness. She had a remarkable embonpoint, and her flesh was as soft as fresh butter and pure as the diamond.

As to her vulva, it was white, prominent, and rounded like a dome; the middle was red and emitted fire; it did not show the least signs of moisture, for, soft to the touch, it was plump and dry. As she walked it stood out in relief, and while she reclined it stretched between her thighs like a child asleep on its mother's breast.

This woman was my neighbour. All the other women played and laughed with me, joked and took pleasure in my fun. I satiated myself with their kisses, caresses, and nibblings, and with

79

sucking their lips, necks and breasts. I tried all except my neighbour, but, above all, I wished to possess her; but she, far from joking with me, avoided me.

One day I went to the house of Fadehat el Jemal. I found her alone as usual. I knocked lightly on her door; she came, beautiful as the day, and said to me:

'Oh, enemy of God, what brings you now?'

'A very important matter, oh mistress mine.'

'Explain it, and I will then see what I can do.'

'I can only explain it when the door is shut.'

'You are very bold to-day.'

'True. Boldness is my strongest point.'

'Oh, enemy of yourself! oh, most despicable of men! If I close the door and you have not got what will satisfy me, what shall I do with you, son of a whore?'

'You will let me share your bed and your favours.'

She laughed and told me to shut the door. I then knew I had gained my end. My member now stood out in front of me like a column. When Fadehat saw it she could not resist; she threw herself onto it, took it in her hands and drew it towards her thighs. I then said:

'Oh, apple of my eye! that must not happen here . . . let us enter your chamber.'

'Do not agitate me, oh son of debauchery! By God! when I see your member stretch itself and lift your clothes, I fear to lose my reason. Oh, what a handsome member! I have never seen a finer! Let it enter this plump, delicious vulva which sends all mad who hear it described, and for which many have died, though few have attained.'

81

'I shall only consent when we are in your room.'

'If you don't do it now I shall surely die.'

As I still insisted that we should go into her room, she exclaimed:

'That is impossible . . . I cannot wait for that!'

Then I saw her lips tremble and her eyes fill with tears. She fell on her back and uncovered her thighs, and their dazzling whiteness made her flesh appear like a crystal tinged with blood.

I then examined her vulva which formed a purple-centred dome. I saw it open and shut like a mare's.

She now grasped my member and, kissing it, said:

'By my father's religion, it must penetrate my vulva.'

Hesitating no longer I placed the head of my member against the lips of her vulva, and she shivered with delight. I listened to her sighs, her moans, and her tears while she held me pressed to her breast.

I took advantage of the moment to again admire the beauties of her vulva. It was magnificent, and its purple centre heightened its dazzling whiteness. It was gently arched and free from the slightest imperfection; it stood above her belly like a graceful dome. Blest be God, the greatest of all creators!

When I saw her so transported and shaking like a frightened bird, I penetrated her with the speed of an arrow. However, thinking she could only accommodate a third of my member, I had taken precautions in consequence. But she madly crissated and cried: 'That is no good!' I

therefore gave a jerk and got right in; she cried aloud and started to crissate with a swinging motion. 'Do not neglect any part, especially the middle. When you feel the moment arrive, let it be in my womb that you may quench my fires.' Then our legs entwined, our muscles relaxed, we kissed and squeezed, and that continued until we simultaneously ejaculated.

I wanted to withdraw my member but she begged me not to; I agreed; then, a moment after, drawing it out herself, she wiped it and replaced it in her vulva. We then began to move again, kissing and embracing the while. Feeling no pleasure this time, we got up and entered her chamber. She gave me a bit of a root, telling me to keep it in my mouth and assuring me that while I kept it there my member would hold up its head. She then told me to lie down and I did so. She mounted onto me and, taking my member in her hand, she thrust it completely into her vagina. I marvelled at her vulva, at the vigor it displayed and the heat it emitted. Her sucker especially aroused my admiration. I had never known its equal; it sucked my member with the greatest ardor, and vigorously bit its head.

Fadehat then was on me; she started to rise and sink, to cry out, to weep, to slacken, to hasten or to cease all movement, and she looked to see if the least bit of my penis was outside her vulva.

We continued our caresses, changing turn and turn about until nightfall. I now thought it advisable to retire but she made me swear to stay.

So I stayed, and all through the night we renewed our caresses.

I reckon that, during that day and night, I performed the act twenty-seven times!

WHEREIN THE WORK IS TERMINATED

Know, oh Vizier (may God grant you His mercy!), that this chapter contains all the most useful information a man of any age can need concerning the best ways of augmenting the sexual powers.

Hear what the wisest and most learned Sheikh has to say to the children of the Most High!

He who will eat every day, after fasting, the yolks of several eggs, will find in this aliment an energetic stimulant of the sexual powers. The same may be said of a diet of yolks and chopped onions continued for three days.

He who will boil some asparagus and then fry it in fat, adding some yolks and powdered condiments, and will eat of this dish every day, will find his desires and powers considerably strengthened.

He who will peel some onions and will put them in a stewpot with condiments and aromatics, then fry this mixture with oil and yolks, will acquire, if he eats some of it during several days, a vigour for coition which will surpass all idea and evaluation.

Camel's milk mixed with honey, if drunk habitually develops an astonishing vigour and keeps the member in erection all day and night.

He who will feed for several days on eggs cooked with myrrh, cinnamon and pepper, will find an increased vigour in his erections and in his capacity for coition. His member will be in such a turgid state that it will seem as if it could never return to a state of repose.

He who wishes to operate a whole night through and who, owing to the suddenness of the desire, has not been able to make the preparations I have already mentioned, will have recourse to the following: he will fry a good number of eggs in fresh fat and butter and, when they are well cooked, he will mix them with honey. If he will eat as much as possible of this with a piece of bread, he will be able to soothe and comfort all through the night.

There are also other drinks of excellent value of which the following is one: Mix a measure of the expressed juice of onions with two measures of clarified honey. Warm over a slow fire until the onion juice has disappeared and only the honey remains. Take off the fire and let cool, then put it by till needed. An ounce of this is mixed with three ounces of water and, in this, pigeon peas are soaked for twenty-four hours. This is drunk in winter and at night, just before

going to bed — a single small dose only being taken. During that night there will be no repose for the member of the man who takes it. If a dose is taken for several consecutive days, the member will remain continuously rigid. A man of ardent temperament should not use the remedy as it may bring on an attack of fever. It is inadvisable to take this remedy for more than three days running, unless one is old or of a cold temperament — in no case should it be taken in summer.

A final tale in which we are reminded of Man's vanity and the folly of jealousy since only Love can be Passion's jailer . . . and all jailers are venal.

There was once a man who had a wife whose beauty was like that of the moon at its full. He was very jealous, for he knew all the tricks that people play. That being so, he never went out without locking the doors of the house and terrasses. One day his wife said to him:

'Why do you do that?'

'Because I know your tricks and habits.'

'What you are doing is no good; when a woman wants a thing, all precautions are useless.'

'Perhaps so! but for all that I'll fasten the doors.'

'Locking a door is no good if a woman has made up her mind to get what you are thinking of.'

'Well! if you can do anything, do it!'

As soon as her husband had gone out, the woman went to the top of the house and made a hole in the wall so that she could see who was passing. At that moment a young man was going along the street; he raised his eyes, saw the woman, and desired to possess her. He asked how he could get to her. She told him he could not enter as all the doors were fastened.

'But how can we meet?' he asked.

'I will make a hole in the house door; you, when you see my husband returning from evening

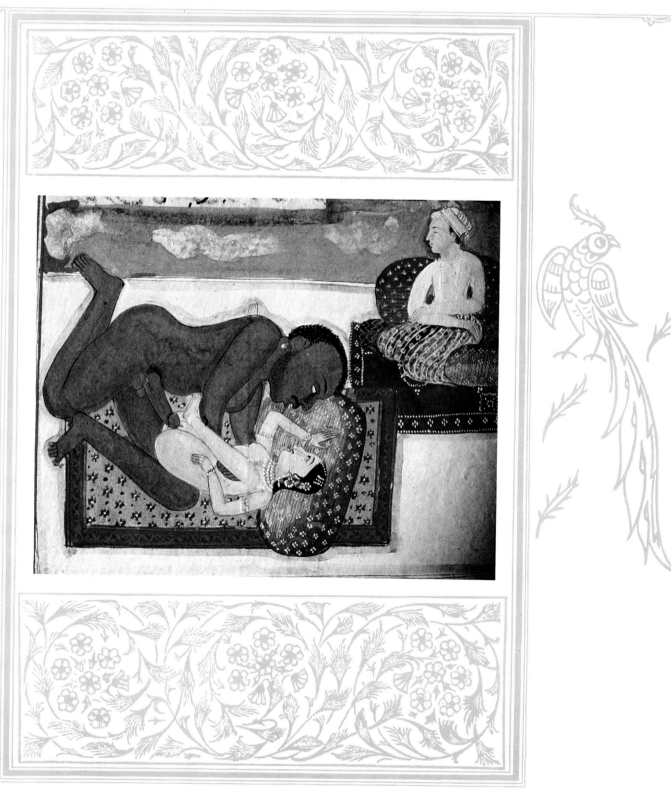

prayer, will wait until he has got inside the house, and then push your member through the hole in the door, opposite which I will put my vulva. In that way we can copulate — any other way will be impossible.'

So the young man watched for the husband's return and, as soon as he had seen him enter the house and close the door behind him, he went to the hole which had been cut in the door and put his member through it. The woman was also on the look-out; hardly had her husband entered, and while he was still in the courtyard, she went to the door under the pretext of seeing if it were fastened; then, hastening to put her vulva opposite the member which was sticking through the hole, she introduced it entirely into her vagina.

That done, she put out her lamp and called to her husband to bring her a light.

'Why?' he asked.

'I have dropped the jewel I wear on my breast and cannot find it.'

So the husband brought a lamp. The young man's member was still in the woman's vulva and it had just ejaculated.

'Where did your jewel fall?' asked the husband.

'There it is!' she cried; and she drew back quickly, leaving uncovered her lover's member, which was withdrawn from the vulva all wet with sperm.

At sight of this the husband fell on the ground in a violent rage and, when he got up, his wife asked:

'Well, what about your precautions?'

'May God make me repent!' was his reply.

In writing this book

I have sinned indeed!

Your pardon, oh Lord, I surely shall need;

But, if on the last day you absolve me, why then,

All my readers will join me

in a loud AMEN!